A Plea for Unity

A Plea for Unity

by
John MacArthur, Jr.

The Master's Communication
P.O. Box 4000
Panorama City, CA 91412

ISBN: 0-8024-5366-X

1 2 3 4 5 6 Printing/LC/Year 94 93 92 91 90

Printed in the United States of America

Contents

These Bible studies are taken from messages delivered by Pastor-Teacher John MacArthur, Jr., at Grace Community Church in Sun Valley, California. These messages have been combined into a 5-tape album titled *A Plea for Unity*. You may purchase this series either in an attractive vinyl cassette album or as individual cassettes. To purchase these tapes, request the album *A Plea for Unity*, or ask for the tapes by their individual GC numbers. Please consult the current price list; then, send your order, making your check payable to:

The Master's Communication
P.O. Box 4000
Panorama City, CA 91412

Or call the following toll-free number:
1-800-55-GRACE

1
Conduct Worthy of the Church

Outline

Introduction
A. The Importance of Worthy Conduct
B. The Imagery Behind Worthy Conduct
C. The Integrity Implied by Worthy Conduct

Lesson
 I. Standing
II. Sharing
   A. Unity Requires a Shared Purity
   B. Unity Requires a Shared Struggle
   C. Unity Requires a Shared Passion
       1. It was Paul's passion
       2. It was Christ's passion
   D. Unity Requires a Shared Humility
   E. Unity Requires a Shared Sacrifice
   F. Unity Requires a Shared Attitude
III. Striving
   A. Unity Requires Teamwork
   B. Unity Requires a Goal
   C. Unity Requires Understanding
   D. Unity Requires Perspective
   E. Unity Requires Assurance
IV. Suffering

Conclusion

Introduction

Philippians 1:27-30 speaks of the church's need to behave according to God's design. Prior to this section Paul's letter is autobiographical—Paul was speaking of his joy in the ministry. In verse 27 he begins to plead with the church. He wanted each member to examine his or her spiritual integrity. That plea also applies to us today.

In Philippians 1:27-30 Paul says, "Only conduct yourselves in a manner worthy of the gospel of Christ; so that whether I come and see you or remain absent, I may hear of you that you are standing firm in one spirit, with one mind striving together for the faith of the gospel; in no way alarmed by your opponents—which is a sign of destruction for them, but of salvation for you, and that too, from God. For to you it has been granted for Christ's sake, not only to believe in Him, but also to suffer for His sake, experiencing the same conflict which you saw in me, and now hear to be in me."

A. The Importance of Worthy Conduct

Paul starts verse 27 with the word "only." It signals he was about to introduce the one essential issue he wanted the Philippians to focus on: living lives worthy of the gospel they believed and proclaimed. That was also Paul's message in Philippians 2:15-16: "Prove yourselves to be blameless and innocent, children of God above reproach in the midst of a crooked and perverse generation, among whom you appear as lights in the world, holding fast the word of life, so that in the day of Christ I may have cause to glory because I did not run in vain nor toil in vain." For Paul the bottom line in church life was behavior worthy of Christ.

B. The Imagery Behind Worthy Conduct

The Greek verb translated "conduct yourselves" in Philippians 1:27 (*politeuō*) refers to behaving as a citizen of a *polis*, a Greek city-state. The English word *political* comes from that term. The Philippians were to conduct themselves as proper citizens of heaven.

Paul's choice of that word was especially appropriate for the Philippian church. Philippi was a Roman colony. That means the citizens of Philippi were citizens of Rome itself (Roman citizenship was highly esteemed in the Roman world), and the city was a small-scale version of Rome. Its citizens were extremely proud of that.

Though Philippi was nearly eight hundred miles from Rome, its citizens reflected the Roman life-style and attitudes. Acts 16 records that when Paul first visited Philippi, Roman citizenship and religion became an issue. It was said of Paul and Silas, "These men are throwing our city into confusion, being Jews, and are proclaiming customs which it is not lawful for us to accept or to observe, being Romans" (vv. 20-21). In Roman colonies the citizens never forgot whom they really belonged to. Rome was their mother—they spoke the language of Rome (Latin), wore Roman dress, and titled their magistrates with Roman names.

To the ancient Greeks, the *polis* was not just a place to live. They took tremendous pride in their cities, viewing their *polis* as a partnership with other people to obtain the highest good for society. People did not live so much for themselves as for the good of the state. Individual citizens developed their abilities, talents, and skills not for their own sake but for the benefit of the community. The success of one citizen reflected on the whole community. Mutuality, interdependence, and the welfare of the state was paramount.

So when Paul instructed the Philippians to live as citizens, they had a vivid picture of what he was talking about. In Philippians 3:20 he says, "Our citizenship is in heaven." As citizens of a heavenly kingdom, believers are to direct their talents, abilities, and endeavors for the good of God's people rather than themselves. Successes are to be on behalf of the community. Behavior is to be governed by the law of God. Righteousness, faith, love, service, and worship are to mark every kingdom citizen. Believers have been delivered out of the domain of darkness into God's kingdom (Col. 1:13). We are enrolled as citizens of heaven (Heb. 12:22-23).

C. The Integrity Implied by Worthy Conduct

The conduct of a kingdom citizen is to be "in a manner worthy of the gospel of Christ" (Phil. 1:27). We are to be consistent with what we believe, teach, and preach. That's what integrity is all about. In our day the church has lost credibility because people professing to be Christians say one thing and do another. When Christians embody their beliefs by their integrity, the gospel is more believable. Integrity is the greatest external weapon the church has.

Too often when the unsaved look at the church, they hear the gospel proclaimed but don't see it lived. Because they don't see professing Christians living lives of holiness, virtue, and salvation from sin, they conclude that the gospel doesn't really accomplish anything. They see immoral pastors, immoral church members, and people who cheat on the job and are untruthful—all of whom profess to be Christians. So when we come to them with the message of deliverance from sin they say, "Oh, really? You Christians don't look delivered."

The "gospel of Christ" (v. 27) refers to the good news of salvation: that people can be saved from sin and made holy. The church must live out the reality of salvation. We are to live as proud citizens of a state far more significant than any earthly state—a heavenly kingdom where Christ reigns and His Word is law. The essence of living according to the gospel is that "if any man is in Christ, he is a new creature; the old things passed away; behold, new things have come" (2 Cor. 5:17).

To his exhortation Paul added, "So that whether I come to see you or remain absent, I may hear of you that you are standing firm" (Phil. 1:27). Paul wanted the Philippians to know that their conduct was not to depend on his presence. That's true in the church today—Christians are not to depend on the presence of their spiritual leaders for spiritual transformation in their lives. Every pastor wants his people to live consistently with the gospel whether he is physically present or not.

It was reasonable for Paul to have such a concern. When he bade farewell to the elders in Ephesus, he said, "I know that after my departure savage wolves will come in among you, not sparing the flock" (Acts 20:29). He wrote to the churches in Galatia, "I am amazed that you are so quickly deserting Him who called you by the grace of Christ, for a different gospel" (Gal. 1:6). Paul wanted the Philippians to live in a worthy manner regardless of his presence.

Lesson

Like a parent telling a child he is going away, Paul instructed the Philippians to behave themselves. They were to do that in four ways.

I. STANDING

Paul wanted the Philippians to stand firm (Phil. 1:27). The Greek word translated "standing firm" (stēkō) refers to the determination of a soldier not to budge from his post (Fritz Rienecker, *A Linguistic Key to the Greek New Testament* [Grand Rapids: Zondervan, 1980], p. 548). Like soldiers, Christians are to be uncompromising in their position, maintaining an unyielding testimony for God's Word and Christ. We are not to be moved either in terms of doctrine or conduct.

Paul said the same thing in Philippians 4:1: "Stand firm in the Lord, my beloved." In both cases Paul used the imperative form of the verb. It's a call for loyalty to the Lord and a demonstration of godliness, purity, virtue, holiness, and obedience. We find the same idea in Ephesians 6:11-13: "Put on the full armor of God, that you may be able to stand firm against the schemes of the devil. . . . Take up the full armor of God, that you may be able to resist in the evil day, and having done everything, to stand firm."

Paul wanted the Philippians to resist the devil, as well as temptation and corruption in doctrine and behavior. The military usage of the word pictures a soldier holding a critical position while under attack. When you're standing spiritually, you're also holding a position under attack. To do that you must have on the full armor of God, "for our struggle is not against flesh and blood, but against the rulers, against the powers, against the world forces of this darkness, against the spiritual forces of wickedness in the heavenly places" (Eph. 6:12). Those phrases are varying descriptions of demonic hosts. First Timothy 4:1 refers to those forces as "deceitful spirits."

Restoring Fallen Leaders

In the church today, many leaders are falling into sin and immorality. Yet what frightens me more than that is the eagerness of various churches to restore these men to leadership. Such action indicates that an entire church—not just a leader—is corrupt. If the corruption were limited only to the leadership, it could be dealt with simply, and the world would know that Christ's church has integrity. But when whole churches allow fallen leaders back into leadership, they show the world that they haven't any more integrity than their leaders. The collapse of the leading soldiers in Christ's army has become epidemic and has spread to the troops at every level.

II. SHARING

Believers do not stand firm on their own—it's a shared experience.

A. Unity Requires a Shared Purity

Philippians 1:27 says we're to be "standing firm in one spirit, with one mind." First, we stand firm in purity, and from that flows the shared experience of oneness in spirit and mind. Purity precedes and produces unity.

B. Unity Requires a Shared Struggle

The battle for unity in the church has been going on since its inception. Paul had to urge the church in Philippi to strive for unity.

1. Philippians 2:1-2—"If . . . there is any encouragement in Christ, if there is any consolation of love, if there is any fellowship of the Spirit, if there is any affection and compassion, make my joy complete by being of the

same mind, maintaining the same love, united in spirit, intent on one purpose."

2. Philippians 4:2—"I urge Euodia and I urge Syntyche to live in harmony in the Lord. Indeed, true comrade, I ask you also to help these women who have shared my struggle."

Discord, disunity, and bitterness persist in the church today. The struggle for unity remains a shared responsibility for all Christians.

C. Unity Requires a Shared Passion

Unity is to be a shared passion among believers.

1. It was Paul's passion

Paul was incessant in his call for unity in the church, as we see in Romans 12:5; 1 Corinthians 1:10; 10:17; Galatians 3:28; Ephesians 2:11-22; and 4:3-4, 13.

2. It was Christ's passion

Christ prayed to the Father that His disciples would be one even as He and the Father were one (John 17:20-21). That was in accord with what He taught them: "By this all men will know that you are My disciples, if you have love for one another" (John 13:35).

D. Unity Requires a Shared Humility

In Philippians 2:3-4 Paul says, "Do nothing from selfishness or empty conceit, but with humility of mind let each of you regard one another as more important than himself; do not merely look out for your own personal interests, but also for the interests of others." Conflict in the church arises when there are at least two people promoting competing interests. That kind of conflict can't exist when everyone is concerned only about the interests of others. When people stop looking out for themselves and start seeking unity, the issue is no longer, "What do I want?" but, "How can I be humble and help others?" Being "right" becomes less important than being unified.

E. Unity Requires a Shared Sacrifice

Now you're not to sacrifice truth, but you need to be willing to forsake your personal preferences. Philippians 2:5 says, "Have this attitude in yourselves which was also in Christ Jesus." Christ had every right to remain in the form of God, but He didn't insist on His rights—He emptied Himself, took the form of a bondservant, and became a man (vv. 6-8). That kind of example shows us the importance of unity; regardless of what we think, want, or prefer, our ideas are to be subservient to the church's unity. Those who make that sacrifice will be blessed by God.

F. Unity Requires a Shared Attitude

Some say that when Paul told the Philippians to stand firm "in one spirit" (v. 27), he was referring to the Holy Spirit. They base their conclusion on 1 Corinthians 12:13, which says, "By one Spirit we were all baptized into one body . . . and we were all made to drink of one Spirit." It's true that the Holy Spirit is the source and power of our unity—Ephesians 4:3 speaks of "the unity of the Spirit in the bond of peace." But in the context of Philippians 1, "spirit" refers to attitude. Paul was saying that a spirit, or attitude, of unity characterizes a godly congregation.

The church is to behave itself. It does that by standing firm—by avoiding error and sin. It also does that by sharing in one spirit and being of one mind. The Greek words Paul used, *pneumati* (spirit) and *psuchē* (mind), refer to the same thing: the immaterial part of man. Sharing, humility, and oneness are to be a part of our inner character. And Paul wanted the Philippians to work for unity regardless of whether he was present.

III. STRIVING

A. Unity Requires Teamwork

The unity of the church is not just for unity's sake. There is a purpose. Philippians 1:27 says we're to be "striving together [Gk., *sunathleō*] for the faith of the gospel." *Sunathleō* means "to struggle along with someone" and pictures a team striving to win a victory. Paul changed the metaphor

14

from that of a soldier standing at his post to a team struggling against a common opponent.

B. Unity Requires a Goal

Unity cannot be maintained in a static situation. Churches that struggle to achieve unity in and of itself, apart from a common goal, never acquire it. The only way to achieve unity is to be engaged in a common struggle to reach a common goal. That's because when everyone is focused on a common goal and desperate to win, no one cares about issues extraneous to obtaining victory.

Perhaps you've read about quarrelsome athletic teams who have nonetheless performed like well-oiled machines when the championship game was on the line. That's because all is forgotten when everyone focuses on a common objective. Generals know what a sense of victory will do to motivate their troops to unity. When the only thing that concerns you is how your side is going to win, the issues of who gets the credit and whether you like the guy next to you become insignificant.

Be a Team Player

When I was in college there was a young man on our basketball team who may have been the finest player in the history of the school. In the opening game he scored about thirty-six points. He carried a thirty-plus average for about ten games but was then kicked off the team. Even though he scored a lot of points, the team couldn't win because he didn't understand what it meant to be part of a team. It was sad because he was so talented. But he was a total failure when it came to accomplishing team goals.

C. Unity Requires Understanding

The church that understands it is engaged in spiritual warfare doesn't find itself caught up in petty disputes that suck away its energy. The only thing that matters is to impact society with the gospel so effectively that the elect receive the truth and are redeemed. Without opponents the unity of the church will be lost. That's why generals and coaches often erect straw men for their men to fight—they would rather they fight an artificial enemy than each other.

When a church sees itself as its own end, it becomes a disaster. The church is a place where believers are trained to go out and reach the world. We live in a world that rejects God and Christ, and it's time for us to stand up and fight that battle. An army that faces death doesn't have any internal quarrels. We are to be concerned only with defeating death by bringing people to Christ. When we acquire that perspective, our petty internal conflicts will dissolve as we strive together.

D. Unity Requires Perspective

Verse 27 says our battle is "for the faith of the gospel." That's the Christian faith—"the faith which was once for all delivered to the saints" (Jude 3). We are in a conflict to preserve and proclaim it. The church needs to remember that it is fighting a twofold battle to achieve a common goal.

Are We Amusing Ourselves to Death?

We live in an age that's tough to reach. A while ago I read a book called *Amusing Ourselves to Death*, by Neil Postman, professor of communication arts and sciences at New York University. He writes, "Today, we must look at the city of Las Vegas, Nevada, as a metaphor of our national character and aspiration. . . . For Las Vegas is a city entirely devoted to the idea of entertainment, and as such proclaims the spirit of a culture in which all public discourse increasingly takes the form of entertainment. Our politics, religion, news, athletics, education and commerce have been transformed into congenial adjuncts of show business, largely without protest or even much popular notice. The result is that we are a people on the verge of amusing ourselves to death" ([New York: Penguin, 1986], pp. 3-4).

Postman believes our culture "is undergoing a vast and trembling shift from the magic of writing to the magic of electronics" (p. 13.). Something put in written form has to be logical and have sufficient content to give proof of what it says. Otherwise it will not be accepted.

16

A society based on print media fosters a cognitive intellectual culture. In such a culture people are willing to stand for seven hours while two men, such as Abraham Lincoln and Steven Douglas, debate each other on complex issues of public policy. Postman asks, "Is there any audience of Americans today who could endure seven hours of talk? or five? or three? Especially without pictures of any kind?" (p. 45). Would any church today stand and listen to the Scriptures being read and explained from dawn till midday (cf. Neh. 8:1-8)? Today we hear thirty-minute sermonettes for Christianettes with histrionics and jokes from beginning to end. Because we've shifted from a typographic to an electronically oriented society, much of public discourse is dangerous nonsense—it lacks logic and content. As a result, the typical TV preacher may say something profound once in thirty minutes, or thirty weeks. There's no reasoned rhetoric or profound logic because he's in competition with explosions, sex, murders, and crashing cars—all available at the touch of a dial.

Of the television preachers, Postman says, "They certainly do not compare favorably with well-known evangelicals of an earlier period, such as Jonathan Edwards, George Whitefield and Charles G. Finney, who were men of great learning, theological subtlety and powerful expositional skills" (p. 117). Jonathan Edwards wrote the *Treatise Concerning Religious Affections* in 1746, one of the most profound American literary works. He often preached by reading his message with no intonation—and people would cry to God for mercy. That's because they had been trained to think. Today a reasoned approach to Scripture quickly puts an audience to sleep. A speaker who knows his audience may be flipping from his channel to a shooting, an explosion, or an announcer saying, "Now this," followed by a trite commercial, is naturally reluctant to engage in carefully reasoned dialogue.

Television trivializes everything, and Christianity is no exception. Someone will preach, and as soon as he's done on comes a commercial cartoon. Even the news is trivialized: an announcer may say, "Today an airliner was shot out of the sky over the Persian Gulf, and 290 people perished. Now this—" and on comes an ad for beer. "The problem is not that television presents us with entertaining subject matter but that all subject matter is presented as entertaining" (p. 87).

When is the last time you heard something on television that changed your life? There can be no Jonathan Edwardses when people demand the kind of emotional gratification television is geared to provide. People don't want to think, and as a result church platforms look increasingly like Las Vegas stages. Vaudeville has replaced the preaching of the Word.

Christianity hasn't been effectively communicated through television in the United States because the medium itself tends to trivialize the gospel. Television is a tremendous challenge to the church because it represents the mind-set of today. Years ago people read books and took time to reflect and think. Those are not characteristic of today's culture.

Beyond the struggle to preserve and propagate God's truth to the outside world is the battle against alleged insiders—shallow churches that trivialize the truth by reducing it to amusement. The struggle for the truth reaches beyond the heart of man; it's a contest for minds as well. We have a mindless generation that wants nothing but entertainment. We can expect the next generation to be worse. And we see the effects of that mind-set in the church today—often when I try to communicate the Word of God over the course of fifty minutes, it simply doesn't sink in.

The Church Cycle of Decline

At Grace Community Church we're in a dangerous time in our history. Win Arn has pointed out that the peak period of growth in large churches is twenty to twenty-five years (message given January 1987 in a series titled "Why Start New Churches?" through Church Growth Incorporated, located in Monrovia, California). That's approximately how long I've been at Grace Community Church. In the churches studied, everything went downhill after that period.

One measure of that decline is the growth rate of a church. When a church is born it takes one person to reach another. Because people are excited and blessed, they replicate themselves. At our church we saw the membership double every two years for about the first ten years. By the third year in the churches studied, it generally took three people to reach one—the process of outreach tends to slow down as a church becomes more complex internally. After ten years it took eight persons to reach another. After fifteen to twenty years it took nearly fifteen people to reach another person. By the time a church was fifty it took eighty-nine to reach just one!

In the early years the churches studied concentrated on evangelism. That evangelistic fervor takes a church to its peak. As time went on, however, the churches slowly began focusing inward instead. They lost their unity because they weren't fighting a common enemy. In their increasing narcissism, evangelism was no longer their reason to exist. They stopped confronting the world and gradually shriveled. So at this time in the history of Grace Community Church we have great reason to be aggressive in our proclamation of the gospel. How about your church?

E. Unity Requires Assurance

In the midst of our struggle we're to be "in no way alarmed by [our] opponents" (Phil. 1:28). That's good news. The word translated "alarmed" is used only here in Scripture but was used in classical Greek to refer to horses that were startled.

Believers are not to be alarmed by their enemies because persecution is a sign that the enemies of God will be destroyed and that believers will be saved. It shows who's on what side.

IV. SUFFERING

We are to expect suffering: "It has been granted for Christ's sake, not only to believe in Him, but also to suffer for His sake" (v. 29). Suffering is a gift of grace. Paul used the verb *charizomai*, which is derived from *charis*—the Greek word for grace. Believers are chosen to receive the gift of suffering. Verse 30 tells us the Philippians were experiencing the same kind of suffering Paul experienced in Philippi (Acts 16:22-24) and Rome (Phil. 1:12-14).

Have you ever regarded suffering as a gift? The health, wealth, and prosperity teachers need to look at this passage. Suffering implies hostility, persecution, animosity, and rejection. It assures us of our salvation, produces the hope of heaven, and makes us more useful in the Lord's service. It provides union with Christ through the fellowship of His sufferings (Phil.

3:10) and the joy of suffering for His sake (Acts 5:41). It leads to eternal reward, strengthens the church, and wins the lost. That's what Paul's suffering did, as he said in Philippians 1:12-14. It ultimately glorifies the Lord.

Conclusion

Every pastor wants to hear that whether he's present with his people or not, they are behaving themselves in a manner worthy of the gospel. That means they're standing firm, one in mind and spirit, and struggling like a team to win the victory. It also means a willingness to suffer hostility from the world. That's what happens in a church that's behaving itself.

Focusing on the Facts

1. Philippians 1:27-30 speaks of the church's need to _____ according to _____ design (see p. 8).
2. What does Paul signal by beginning Philippians 1:27 with the word "only" (see p. 8)?
3. What does the Greek verb *politeuō* refer to? What would that have reminded the Philippians of (see pp. 8-9)?
4. Believers are to be consistent with what they _____ , _____ , and _____ (see p. 10).
5. What is the greatest external weapon the church has (see p. 10)?
6. What is the essence of living according to the gospel (2 Cor. 5:17; see p. 10)?
7. Paul wanted the Philippians to live in a worthy manner regardless of _____ _____ (see p. 11).
8. What does "standing firm" in Philippians 1:27 refer to? What does that mean in terms of the Christian's testimony (see p. 11)?
9. What does the rush to restore fallen leaders in the church indicate about a church as a whole (see p. 12)?
10. The importance of the issue of unity in the church can be seen in the many times it is called for in _____ (see p. 13).
11. What metaphors did Paul use in Philippians 1:27 (see pp. 14-15)?
12. Why is it important that a church understand the goal it is striving for (see pp. 15-16)?
13. According to Neil Postman, what are we on the verge of doing in the United States? How does that affect Christianity (see pp. 16-17)?

14. What causes loss of unity in a church (see p. 19)?
15. Why shouldn't believers be alarmed by their enemies (Phil. 1:28; see p. 19)?
16. Why should a church expect to suffer (Phil. 1:29-30; see pp. 19-20)?

Pondering the Principles

1. The Puritan Thomas Watson wrote, "There is but one God, and they that serve him should be one. There is nothing that would render the true religion more lovely . . . than to see the professors of it tied together with the heart-strings of love" (*A Body of Divinity* [Edinburgh: Banner of Truth Trust, 1958 reprint], pp. 107-8). Christian love resulting in unity ought to be the norm— the apostle John said it is a sign of saving faith (1 John 3:10). Are you striving to achieve unity with your brothers and sisters in Christ?

2. Puritan John Trapp rightly said, "Unity without verity [truth] is no better than conspiracy" (cited in *The Golden Treasury of Puritan Quotations* [I. D. E. Thomas, ed. Edinburgh: Banner of Truth Trust, 1977], p. 304). Christian unity requires a unity that is Christian, a unity based on the essential truths of the Christian faith. Are you seeking unity in accordance with the truths of God's Word?

3. We have seen the increasing tendency of churches to excuse pastors and other church leaders who fall into sin. It is incorrectly assumed that the leaders of the church are just like other church members and therefore ought to be similarly restored. But Richard Baxter, writing to pastors in the seventeenth century, said, "Your sins have more heinous aggravations than other men's. . . . O what treachery is it to make such a stir against [sin] in the pulpit, and, after all, to entertain it in thy heart, and give it the room that is due to God, and even prefer it before the glory of the saints!" (*The Reformed Pastor* [Edinburgh: Banner of Truth Trust, 1974 reprint], pp. 76-77). A leader who is not above reproach has lost his ability to lead God's people (cf. 1 Tim. 3:2) because his warnings against sin will be received with skepticism. What is your response to the failures of leadership in the church today?

2
The Motives for Spiritual Unity

Outline

Introduction
A. The Philippians Had a Special Church
B. The Philippians Had Special Leaders
C. The Philippians Had a Special Problem

Lesson
I. The Motives for Unity (vv. 1-2*a*)
A. The Encouragement We Have in Christ
B. The Love We Have in Christ
C. The Fellowship We Have in the Spirit
D. The Affection and Compassion We Have in the Spirit
1. Affection
2. Compassion
E. The Spiritual Relationship We Have with Our Church Leaders

Conclusion

Introduction

A. The Philippians Had a Special Church

Paul had a special place in his heart for the congregation at Philippi. They apparently felt the same way about him. Paul began by saying, "I thank my God in all my remembrance of you" (1:3). He prayed for them with joy (v. 4), was grateful for their participation in the gospel (v. 5), and longed for them "with the affection of Christ Jesus" (v. 8).

Philippians 1:19 mentions the church's prayers on Paul's behalf, and 2:12 mentions their constant obedience. They had attained a high standard of Christian living. Paul urged them to continue living up to it (3:16). He rejoiced greatly in the Lord because they had shown their concern for him by sending a generous offering (4:10)—and that wasn't the first time (4:16).

B. The Philippians Had Special Leaders

The Philippians had special leaders. Paul mentioned "the overseers and deacons" at the outset of his letter. In 1:5 he affirms their genuineness and in 1:7 their great courage: the leadership in Philippi had stood by Paul as partakers of grace, even when he was imprisoned. Philippians 1:9 indicates they had a love that would abound yet more and more.

C. The Philippians Had a Special Problem

The letter to the Philippians lacks overt doctrinal exhortations because the church apparently hadn't deviated doctrinally. But in spite of their apparent doctrinal purity, a deadly snake with poisonous venom lurked in the church: that of disunity, discord, and conflict. It has poisoned many churches. That snake was of grave concern to Paul. The entire letter is centered on that issue.

In Philippians 1:27 Paul tells the Philippians to stand firm "in one spirit, with one mind striving together for the faith of the gospel." In chapter 4 we see him urging two women "to live in harmony in the Lord" (v. 2). In chapter 2 Paul speaks of the prime example of church unity: Jesus Christ. From beginning to end Paul's letter to the Philippians is a plea for unity.

My constant prayer for Grace Community Church is that we not be torn apart by disunity. That is something every godly church needs to be vigilant about. Commentator William Barclay wrote, "There is a sense in which [disunity] is the danger of every healthy church. It is when people are really in earnest and their beliefs really matter to them, that they are apt to get up against each other. The greater their enthusiasm, the greater the danger that they may collide" (*The Letters to the Philippians, Colossians, and Thessalonians*, rev. ed.

[Philadelphia: Westminster, 1975], p. 31). True doctrine and zealous members do not preclude the possibility of discord.

Marbles and Magnets

Scripture exhorts us to a unity that is internally compelling, not externally controlled. It's more heartfelt than creedal. It's more spiritual than verbal. It's the union of hearts, minds, and souls in common cause—a union of people attracted to each other because they're motivated by the same power.

A bag filled with marbles represents a certain kind of unity. There's one bag, it's full of marbles, and all those marbles are packed together. But the bag is the only thing keeping them together. Tear it, and the marbles will go everywhere because there's nothing else binding them together.

Now picture a magnet laid on a pile of metal shavings. The shavings adhere to the magnet. They aren't held together by an external container but by an internal force that pulls them all together. That's how the church is to be—not a collection of marbles in a bag but people drawn together by a common force: Jesus Christ.

That kind of magnetic unity is essential to a church's joy and effectiveness. It pictures true unity of the Spirit—a precious yet fragile commodity. Ephesians 4:3 says we're to be "endeavoring to keep the unity of the Spirit in the bond of peace" (KJV*). The Greek word translated "endeavoring" (*spoudazō*) speaks of making every effort. Unity requires tremendous and constant effort.

Lesson

Philippians 2:1-4 says, "If therefore there is any encouragement in Christ, if there is any consolation of love, if there is any fellowship of the Spirit, if any affection and compassion, make my joy complete by being of the same mind, maintaining the same love, united in spirit, intent on one purpose. Do nothing from selfishness or empty conceit, but with humility of mind let each of you regard one another as more important than himself; do not merely look

*King James Version.

25

out for your own personal interests, but also for the interests of others."

Paul introduced the subject of unity in Philippians 1:27-30. In 2:1-8 he gives us insight into the elements of that unity: the motives, marks, means, and model. Philippians 2:1 begins with "therefore" because the following verses are based on Paul's plea in 1:27-30.

The heart of Philippians 2:1-4 is the phrase "being of the same mind" (v. 2). Paul said the same thing in Philippians 1:27: the church was to be of one spirit and one mind, striving together. In 2:1-4 Paul explains why he wants them to be of one mind, what he means, and how they can do so.

I. THE MOTIVES FOR UNITY (vv. 1-2a)

"If therefore there is any encouragement in Christ, if there is any consolation of love, if there is any fellowship of the Spirit, if any affection and compassion, make my joy complete by being of the same mind."

Philippians 2:1 gives us the motives for maintaining unity within the church: the encouragement and love we have in Christ; the fellowship, affection, and compassion we have in the Spirit; and the spiritual relationship we have with our church leaders. Each motive is preceded by the word *if* in the English text, which indicates a first-class condition in the Greek text. A more extended translation might read, "If (and it is true)" or, "if (as in fact it is)." Other kinds of conditional clauses could be translated, "if (and it might be true)" or, "if (and it is possibly true)"— but a first-class condition could not be translated in those ways. Possibly the clearest translation of a first-class condition is to use the word *since*. Thus, Philippians 2:1 would read, "[Since] there is encouragement in Christ, [since] there is consolation of love." Another word that could be used is *because*. Paul was saying that because of those varying motivations the Philippians ought to be compelled toward unity. He was not speaking of doctrinal abstractions but of motivations within the spiritual experience of the Philippians.

A. The Encouragement We Have in Christ

"Encouragement in Christ" is our first motive for unity. The Greek word translated "encouragement" (*paraklēsis*) means

26

"to come alongside and help, encourage, counsel, exhort."
The Holy Spirit is our Paraclete (John 14:26) because He
comes alongside and helps believers. Paul was saying that
those who are in Christ have experienced His help. He has
come alongside you and has encouraged, exhorted, coun-
seled, and helped you. That should lead you to be of the
same mind toward your brothers and sisters in Christ.

The great blessings of Christ's constant forgiveness, strength,
and wisdom ought to create unity. After all, He prayed that
believers be one as He and the Father were (John 17:20-21).
In John 13:35 Jesus says, "By this all men will know that you
are My disciples, if you have love for one another." Our
Lord's great passion was the unity of His people. His ongo-
ing influence in our lives—His gentle encouragement, exhortation, and counsel from the moment of salvation—
ought to spur us to give back to Christ what is precious to
His heart.

That means obedience needs to replace selfishness. Obedience to Christ should be the natural response to our relationship with Him. When we sin, we are not just violating a
system of religion, theology, or organization. We are violating the intimacy of our relationship with Christ. Discord in
the church violates the church's relationship to the Head of
the church—Jesus Christ. Factiousness denies Christ what is
rightfully due Him in light of all He has given us.

B. The Love We Have in Christ

The "consolation of love" referred to in Philippians 2:1 is the
loving tenderness of God in Christ experienced by every
Christian. We know the comfort of God's forgiveness, mercy, and grace. Because He has given to us so abundantly, it
ought to be our natural response to seek what is precious to
His heart: the unity of His people.

I believe that Paul's first two motivations for unity relate to
Christ and the second two to the Holy Spirit. The first motivation (encouragement in Christ) mentions Christ, and the
second flows from it. The third (the fellowship of the Spirit)
mentions the Holy Spirit, and the fourth flows out of that.

The Greek word in Philippians 2:1 translated "consolation" (*paramuthion*) speaks of gentle cheering or tender counsel. It depicts an individual coming close and whispering in another's ear and is used in the New Testament in the context of friendship and intimate love.

The Greek word translated "love" (*agape*) describes the greatest kind of love—the love of choice, apart from the worthiness of the object loved. Because Christians are constantly encouraged in our relationship to Christ by His coming alongside to speak words of friendship and love, we ought to be compelled to give back to Him what He longs for: our unity.

Paul spoke with gentleness to the Philippians. He was not abusive, judgmental, or threatening. The plea of his heart was that, by remembering the love and encouragement of Christ, they would be moved toward unity. In his plea is an implied question: Can you take all that from Christ and not give back to Him what is most precious to His heart? Those who refuse to work toward unity violate their relationship with Him. Such is the betrayal of a familiar friend—like the betrayal of Judas.

C. The Fellowship We Have in the Spirit

"Fellowship" (Gk., *koinonia*) refers to partnership, communion, and sharing. The Holy Spirit desires unity—the unity of the church is called "the unity of the Spirit" (Eph. 4:3). We have all been baptized by the Spirit into one Body and made to drink of the same Spirit (1 Cor. 12:13). We're the temple of God, and the Holy Spirit lives inside us (1 Cor. 3:16). The Spirit desires unity, is the source of unity, and is in fellowship with every believer.

Our fellowship with the Spirit means we are the beneficiaries of all that our union with Him can provide. Believers are sealed by the Spirit (Eph. 1:13-14), and He serves as the guarantor of our eternal inheritance. He fills us and empowers us for service. We are gifted by the Spirit (1 Cor. 12:7) and continually cleansed by Him. The Spirit prays for us with groanings that cannot be uttered (Rom. 8:26). We often do not know the will of God for a specific situation and therefore are at a loss on how to pray, but the Spirit knows God's will and makes the appropriate intercession for us.

The Spirit has effected our regeneration and sanctification, guarantees our eternal glory, unceasingly prays for us, gives us gifts, fills us, produces fruit in us, teaches us, enables us to resist temptation, gives us the Word, fills us with holy impulses, and has given us everything pertaining to life and godliness. Therefore we are to give Him what He desires: unity in the church.

Disunity violates our relationship with the Spirit. It quenches Him (1 Thess. 5:19) and shows Him contempt (Eph. 4:30). He who violates the unity of the church in effect says, "I will take all the Spirit gives, but won't give anything back to Him." Such sin in the life of a Christian is a tragic act of ingratitude. It accepts grace upon grace and mercy upon mercy, but defies the desire of both Christ and the Spirit.

D. The Affection and Compassion We Have in the Spirit

1. Affection

"Affection" (Gk., *splanchnon*) refers to the viscera. It was commonly translated "bowels" in older Bible versions and refers metaphorically to deep affection. It's where we experience emotion. The Holy Spirit has a deep affection for believers. The first-class condition in the Greek text means we have received His deeply felt longing and affection for us. He has given what He longs for us to have.

God isn't a cold, hard, indifferent deity who functions like a machine, spitting out good things on those who are Christians. Ours is a living relationship with a Savior who encourages, exhorts, and ministers to us. When we fall, He picks us up. When we sin, He forgives us. He gives us strength and wisdom because He loves us.

The same is true of our relationship with the Spirit. He isn't a floating fog that mystically makes things happen. He is a Person who lives in every believer and longs to bless us. Through God's grace we have experienced His blessing.

2. Compassion

Paul used the Greek word translated "compassion" (*oiktirmos*) four times in his epistles. Twice it is translated "mercies" (Rom. 12:1; 2 Cor. 1:3) and the other two times "compassion" (Phil. 2:1; Col. 3:12). We have received the longings of the Spirit and the tender, compassionate mercy of God, which is also given through the Spirit.

According to Paul, the compassion God shows us ought to result in unity in the church. That's what He desires. Too often during disagreements in the church people think, *I'm going to get my pound of flesh. I think this is the way we need to go, and I'm going to do it!* Divisiveness is a terrible disloyalty both to Christ and to the Spirit, who long for the unity of the church.

But Paul didn't resort to threats to encourage unity. He didn't act like the father who says to his son, "You've got two hours to change your conduct or you're out of this house for good, and I'm serious!" Nor did he act like the father who says, "I'll thrash you within an inch of your life so you'll never forget it! That'll teach you a lesson!"

Stern warnings and spankings aren't wrong when properly applied. But unlike his approach with the Corinthians (1 Cor. 4:21), Paul didn't threaten the Philippians—he was tender with them. He was like the father who sits down with his son and says, "Haven't your mother and I loved you faithfully in this family? Haven't we encouraged you? When you were sad, didn't we come alongside you to offer you compassion and care and sympathy? When you were hungry, didn't we provide food for you? Didn't we clothe you? Didn't we nurture you as you grew from a little child? Didn't we provide all the medical care you needed to live a healthy life? Didn't we give you a warm environment to live in? A bed to sleep in? Son, haven't we shown you deep affection? Haven't we been gracious to you in the times when you were disobedient and rebellious, always quick to forgive and restore you?

Haven't we shown you mercy? Haven't we been patient with you while you were learning to do things right (and often did them wrong)? Haven't you experienced our goodness to you? Son, since all those things are true, isn't it reasonable for us to ask you to live in such a way that will bring us joy?" It would be pretty hard for a child to deny his parents their joy if all of those things were true.

Paul's plea was based on God's goodness. He took a gentle approach with the Philippians because they were a particularly good church. Unfortunately, that approach can't always be taken because not all people live on as high a plane as the Philippians.

E. The Spiritual Relationship We Have with Our Church Leaders

In Philippians 2:2 Paul adds one more motivation for unity: the church's relationship to him personally. He wrote, "Make my joy complete by being of the same mind." That must have tugged at their hearts. It's as if he said, "In addition to being united for the sake of Christ and the Holy Spirit, do it for my sake."

That's a warm thought. He spoke as a pastor who personally yearned for unity among his people. I understand why he said that. My greatest fear for the church is disunity. My own joy would be complete if the church were unified by being of the same mind. Hebrews 13:17 says, "Obey your leaders, and submit to them; for they keep watch over your souls, as those who will give an account. Let them do this with joy and not with grief." It's legitimate to give the leadership of the church the joy of biblical unity. Paul desired that for the Philippians because of his deep affection for them (cf. Phil. 1:8).

Conclusion

There is pathos in Paul's plea. He was a prisoner in Rome and didn't know whether he would live or die. When the Philippians heard of his imprisonment, their hearts were broken. They were worried that Paul would be brokenhearted and despondent, so they sent Epaphroditus to care for Paul and bring him a generous gift (4:18). Epaphroditus did his job so well it nearly killed him (2:25-30). Paul sent Epaphroditus back to Philippi with his letter telling them he was rejoicing and that they shouldn't worry. In that context Paul said they would make his joy complete by maintaining unity. That's the pinnacle of the epistle. Paul was rejoicing, but he would rejoice more if the Philippians would maintain their unity.

Every pastor fears disunity in the church and strives to keep the flock together. Unity is a practical necessity. Those who have received the encouragement of Christ, the consolation of His love, and the fellowship and affection of the Spirit should reciprocate by doing everything possible to promote unity in the church.

Focusing on the Facts

1. Describe the way in which the Philippian church was special to Paul (see pp. 23-24).
2. What special problem lurked in the church at Philippi (see p. 24)?
3. Why is disunity a danger for every healthy church (see p. 24)?
4. A church with true doctrine and zealous people does not preclude the possibility of _____ (see pp. 24-25).
5. What kind of unity does Scripture exhort us to (see p. 25)?
6. _____ requires tremendous and constant effort (see p. 25).
7. What is the heart of Philippians 2:1-4 (see p. 26)?
8. What motives do we have for maintaining unity within the church (see p. 26)?
9. What possibilities exist for translating a first-class condition from Greek to English? What did Paul mean by his use of first-class condition clauses in Philippians 2:1 (see p. 26)?
10. What does the Greek word translated "encouragement" (*paraklēsis*) mean (see pp. 26-27)?
11. What was our Lord's great passion (see p. 27)?
12. What does sin violate (see p. 27)?
13. What is the "consolation of love" referred to in Philippians 2:1 (see p. 27)?
14. To whom do the first two motivations for unity relate in Philippians 2:1? To whom do the second two relate (see p. 27)?
15. What does our fellowship with the Spirit mean (see p. 28)?

16. The Holy Spirit has deep _____ for believers (see p. 29).
17. The compassion God shows us should result in what(see p. 30)?
18. What was Paul's method for encouraging unity among the Philippians (see p. 30-31)?
19. It's legitimate to give the leadership of the church the joy of _____ (see p. 31).

Pondering the Principles

1. How far will love for Christ go to preserve the unity of the church? Thomas Watson wrote, "Love is a humble grace; it does not walk abroad in state; it will creep upon its hands; it will stoop and submit to anything whereby it may be serviceable to Christ" (*All Things for Good* [Edinburgh: Banner of Truth Trust, 1986 reprint], p. 87). If unity means giving up your own prerogatives for another so that Christ may obtain what He desires, will you stoop that low to please Him?

2. Many in the church today think unity means compromise. The American pastor A. W. Tozer wrote, "The constantly recurring question must be: What shall we unite with and from what shall we be separate? The question of coexistence does not enter here, but the question of union and fellowship does. The wheat grows in the same field with the tares, but shall the two cross-pollinate? The sheep graze near the goats, but shall they seek to interbreed? The unjust and the just enjoy the same rain and sunshine, but shall they forget their deep moral differences and intermarry? . . . The Spirit-illuminated church will have none of this" (*The Best of A. W. Tozer* [Harrisburg, Pa.: Christian Publications, 1978], p. 72). Unity apart from compromise comes only when the church strives together according to a common standard—God's Word. Are you striving for unity or compromise?

3
The Marks of Spiritual Unity

Outline

Introduction
A. The Importance of Unity
B. The Reason for Unity

Review
 I. The Motives for Unity (vv. 1-2*a*)

Lesson
II. The Marks of Unity (v. 2*b*)
   A. Being of the Same Mind
      1. Think about spiritual things
      2. Exercise sound judgment
      3. Think like Christ
      4. Let Scripture dwell richly within you
      5. Be filled with the Spirit
   B. Maintaining the Same Love
   C. Being United in Spirit
   D. Being of One Purpose

Conclusion
A. The Evidence of Unity
      1. People who think alike
      2. People who love each other
      3. People who have like passions
B. The Crisis Threatening Unity

Introduction

What I most fear in the church is disunity. I believe that in my own church, and in many others in our country, disunity is the major attack the enemy is making against us. Acts 4:32 says, "The congregation of those who believed were of one heart and soul." As a result of that unity the apostles witnessed with great power, "and abundant grace was upon them all" (v. 33). Power and blessing are by-products of unity.

A. The Importance of Unity

The unity of the church was a priority with Jesus. It was so important to Paul that he wrote in Philippians 2:1-4, "If . . . there is any encouragement in Christ, if there is any consolation of love, if there is any fellowship of the Spirit, if any affection and compassion, make my joy complete by being of the same mind, maintaining the same love, united in spirit, intent on one purpose. Do nothing from selfishness or empty conceit, but with humility of mind let each of you regard one another as more important than himself; do not merely look out for your own personal interests, but also for the interests of others."

That is perhaps the most concise and practical explanation of unity given in the New Testament. It flows out of Paul's exhortation for the Philippians to stand firm "in one spirit, with one mind striving together for the faith of the gospel" (1:27).

B. The Reason for Unity

Paul's thoughts in Philippians 2:1-4 are echoed in Ephesians 4:1-6: "I . . . entreat you to walk in a manner worthy of the calling with which you have been called, with all humility and gentleness, with patience, showing forbearance to one another in love, being diligent to preserve the unity of the Spirit in the bond of peace. There is one body and one Spirit, just as you were also called in one hope of your calling; one Lord, one faith, one baptism, one God and Father of all who is over all and through all and in all." The unity we are called to is based on the unity of the Trinity itself: one Spirit, one Lord, and one Father.

Review

I. THE MOTIVES FOR UNITY (vv. 1-2*a*; see pp. 26-32)

A. The Encouragement We Have in Christ (see pp. 26-27)

B. The Love We Have in Christ (see pp. 27-28)

C. The Fellowship We Have in the Spirit (see pp. 28-29)

D. The Affection and Compassion We Have in the Spirit (see pp. 29-31)

E. The Spiritual Relationship We Have with Our Church Leaders (see p. 31)

First Thessalonians 5:12-15 says, "We request . . . that you appreciate those who diligently labor among you, and have charge over you in the Lord and give you instruction [their shepherds, or pastors], and that you esteem them very highly in love because of their work. Live in peace with one another . . . admonish the unruly, encourage the faint-hearted, help the weak, be patient with all men. See that no one repays another with evil for evil, but always seek after that which is good for one another and for all men." You please your church leaders by seeking unity.

Gratitude and love for Christ, the Spirit, and one's own spiritual leaders lead to unity of heart and mind. Discord in the church is sin against all three. Knowing that ought to be motive enough for unity.

Lesson

II. THE MARKS OF UNITY (v. 2*b*)

"[Be] of the same mind, maintaining the same love, united in Spirit, intent on one purpose."

In that verse we see four marks of spiritual unity. They tend to overlap, but each is distinctive.

A. Being of the Same Mind

"Of the same mind" (Gk., *phroneō*) means "to think the same way." A key to unity is thinking alike.

The book of 1 Corinthians was written to a factional church. Paul described the Corinthians as "still fleshly" (1 Cor. 3:3) because of their many divisions. His first exhortation to them after introducing his letter was, "I exhort you . . . that you all agree, and there be no divisions among you, but you be made complete in the same mind and in the same judgment" (1 Cor. 1:10). Then he dealt with the specific divisions that had been reported to him. Likemindedness among believers is not an optional or obscure issue. Its necessity is repeated throughout Scripture. Unity comes when believers think alike.

When Paul exhorted the Philippians to be unified, he was not talking about doctrine. Many Christians subscribe to the same doctrinal statements but do not think alike. Paul was concerned with attitude. He wanted them to have the same mind-set, or disposition. In Philippians 2:5 he says, "Have this *attitude* in yourselves which was also in Christ Jesus" (emphasis added). He emphasizes the need for right attitude again in 3:15. In 3:19 he notes that the ungodly have "set their minds on earthly things"—their attitudes are controlled by earthly desires. He was speaking of the bent of one's mind—the orientation of one's feelings, disposition, and thinking patterns. Believers are to have a common understanding.

Likemindedness can't be orchestrated by fleshly means. Over the years I have seen that human beings are incapable of orchestrating that kind of unity. It can be achieved only on a divine level. Beyond that, we will never know and wholeheartedly do the will of God until we think alike.

Conflict invariably results when people don't think alike. In Philippians we don't find allusions to doctrinal or ethical problems, but we do see a problem with unity in attitude.

How does a church attain unity of attitude?

1. Think about spiritual things

   Romans 8:4-6 says Christians are those "who do not walk according to the flesh, but according to the Spirit. For those who are according to the flesh set their minds on the things of the flesh, but those who are according to the Spirit, [set their minds on] the things of the Spirit. For the mind set on the flesh is death, but the mind set on the Spirit is life and peace." The Greek word translated "set their minds on" in Philippians 2:2 is the same one that describes likemindedness.

   A person can either think on the things of the Spirit or of the flesh. As a church we must all think spiritual thoughts. We need to turn our minds away from the flesh—what the Puritans called indwelling or abiding sin, the part of every Christian that is to be mortified. Conflict in the church is always between the Spirit and the flesh—never between the Spirit and the Spirit. Two people thinking on the things of the Spirit can't be in conflict. In situations of conflict, one party is always dwelling on the flesh.

2. Exercise sound judgment

   In Romans 12:3 Paul says, "Through the grace given to me I say to every man among you not to think more highly of himself than he ought to think; but to think so as to have sound judgment, as God has allotted to each a measure of faith." We're to use sound, divine judgment. That means we're to think objectively. We get into trouble when we think subjectively. Discord develops at all levels of relationships because often Christians don't think objectively. When we focus on our private agendas, priorities, and ambitions, pride will compel us toward evil ends.

3. Think like Christ

   a) Romans 15:5—"May the God who gives perseverance and encouragement grant you to be of the same mind [or attitude] with one another according to Christ Jesus."

b) 1 Corinthians 2:16—"Who has known the mind of the Lord, that he should instruct Him? But we have the mind of Christ." Believers have the mind of Christ and can therefore think the thoughts of Christ and have a Christlike attitude. Yet Paul said to the Corinthian church that he "could not speak to [them] as to spiritual men, but as to men of flesh" (3:1). Their condition had come about because of jealousy and strife—they were walking about like mere men (3:3). They had the mind of man, not Christ.

c) 2 Corinthians 13:11-13—"Rejoice, be made complete [or mature], be comforted, be like-minded, live in peace; and the God of love and peace . . . the grace of the Lord Jesus Christ . . . and the fellowship of the Holy Spirit [shall] be with you all." Those who are spiritually mature are in harmony with the mind of the Trinity.

d) Colossians 3:2—"Set your mind on the things above, not on the things that are on earth." That was the focus of Christ.

4. Let Scripture dwell richly within you

Colossians 3:12-16 says, "As those who have been chosen of God, holy and beloved, put on a heart of compassion, kindness, humility, gentleness and patience; bearing with one another, and forgiving each other, whoever has a complaint against anyone; just as the Lord forgave you, so also should you. And beyond all these things, put on love, which is the perfect bond of unity. And let the peace of Christ rule in your hearts, to which indeed you were called in one body; and be thankful. *Let the word of Christ richly dwell within you*, with all wisdom teaching and admonishing one another with psalms and hymns and spiritual songs, singing with thankfulness in your hearts to God" (emphasis added).

Right relationships will exist in the church when Scripture is the dominating and energizing force in the lives of its members. When the Word of Christ dwells richly within you, your instincts and involuntary reactions will be right. There's nothing mystical about unity—it's a matter of letting the Word of Christ dominate you.

5. Be filled with the Spirit

Ephesians 5:18-20 says, "Do not get drunk with wine, for that is dissipation, but be filled with the Spirit, speaking to one another in psalms and hymns and spiritual songs, singing and making melody with your heart to the Lord; always giving thanks for all things in the name of our Lord Jesus Christ." The rich indwelling of Scripture and being filled with the Spirit have the same result.

The members of the Trinity desire unity in the church. Conflict results from failing to think on a divine level and addressing relationships in the church from one's own fleshly agenda. It follows those who are quick to speak and slow to think, pray, meditate, and search the mind of God.

B. Maintaining the Same Love

The second principle flows from the first. Those who are of the same mind maintain the same love. They love everyone the same. Since no one can be equally attracted emotionally to everyone, we may conclude that Paul meant something other than emotional attachment. Scripture reveals that we're to show our love for others by serving them sacrificially.

1. Romans 12:10—"Be devoted to one another in brotherly love."

2. John 15:13—"Greater love has no one than this, that one lay down his life for his friends."

3. 1 John 3:17—"Whoever has the world's goods, and beholds his brother in need and closes his heart against him, how does the love of God abide in him?" Love acts to meet another's need.

4. John 3:16—"God so loved the world, that He gave His only begotten Son, that whosoever believes in Him should not perish, but have eternal life." God provided

41

what man so desperately needed through the sacrifice of His Son. That kind of love is an element of unity.

Those who think about spiritual things, exercise sound judgment, and think like Christ will maintain the same love. That's because Christ and the Spirit love through, and produce love among, such people.

People in the church clash because they fail to maintain unity of attitude, and that means a failure to maintain love. Regardless of who the people are, conflict comes when they feel something other than love for each other. That can result in bitterness, envy, jealousy, personal ambition, defensiveness, possessiveness, and hostility. Those are loveless attitudes. Ask the Spirit of God to fill your heart with surpassing spiritual love for all who are in the Body of Christ.

C. Being United in Spirit

The Greek word translated "united in spirit" (*sumpsuchoi*) in Philippians 2:2 is used only here in the New Testament. Paul may have coined the term himself. It means "one-souled" and carries the flavor of the modern term "soul brother." Such people are knit together in harmony—their passions, desires, and ambitions are the same. People like that are united in spirit.

When one person's greatest desire is to serve God in the Spirit and another person desires to be prominent, disunity will result. When someone has a heartfelt hunger to see Christ's church united and another wants the whole world to know he's been offended, people will collide. Those who concentrate on how they've been injured will react in the flesh, and soon their minds deceive them with imagined hurts that are purely a product of their fleshly minds. That can destroy the unity of a church.

A driving passion for unity of spirit and the glory of God will bring about unity in the church. But defensiveness, possessiveness, personal ambition, jealousy, pride, taking offense, and unrealistic feelings of persecution will destroy the "one-souled" nature of a church.

D. Being of One Purpose

Oneness of passion will result in oneness of purpose. Often people in conflict have not stopped to examine their purposes. A group of people who have different purposes are going to have a lot of problems. In contrast, Philippians 2:2 says we're to be "intent on one purpose." That phrase amplifies the meaning of "being of the same mind." We're to be of the same mind by being intent on one purpose—advancing the kingdom.

Being of one mind leads to an equality of love and service. That kind of love is accompanied by a single passion for unity. Personal agendas are put aside as the church moves toward its one eternal and glorious purpose.

Conclusion

In Philippians 2:2 Paul is saying the same thing in different ways. The marks of unity overlap. Philippians 2:2 ought to result in a deep desire for unity.

A. The Evidence of Unity

1. People who think alike

Unity characterizes a group of people who think alike. The church is to be characterized by a deep knowledge of the Word of Christ energized by the Spirit's power. By continually walking in the Spirit, the church will maintain the same spiritual attitude of unity.

2. People who love each other

Unity is evidenced in a group of people who love and serve each other equally. They don't hold grudges and do not react with anger because of a supposed offense.

3. People who have like passions

Those who feel a like passion toward the same holy principles, goals, and divine ends will demonstrate unity.

They're compelled from the inside to accomplish things unrelated to themselves.

B. The Crisis Threatening Unity

I am concerned about the church because I believe our society has been producing selfish, self-indulgent, egotistical, introverted, consumptive, materialistic people. The spillover from that has had a devastating impact on the church. Too often professing Christians are hostile, angry people. To a great extent, the church has accepted the "do your own thing" philosophy of the culture around it. As a result, many of us have come to know little of the Bible's command to seek oneness and give of ourselves for one another. The legacy of our warped, pagan, and godless culture is a generation given over to the monster of self-indulgence. That's a frightening threat to the church.

I pray God will put a halt to that trend for the sake of His name and the purity of His church. But the church has no excuse, no matter what popular culture dictates. Ours isn't the first culture given over to self-indulgence, and, if the Lord tarries, it won't be the last. But the Word of God still binds His people to the responsibility of seeking unity.

Focusing on the Facts

1. _____ and _____ are the by-products of unity (see p. 36).
2. What reason did Paul give for behaving in a way that promotes unity (Eph. 4:1-6; see p. 36)?
3. What should gratitude and love for Christ, the Spirit, and one's spiritual leaders result in (see p. 37)?
4. What does the Greek verb *phroneō* mean (see p. 38)?
5. True or false—When Paul exhorted the Philippians to unity he was talking about doctrinal issues (see p. 38). Explain your answer.
6. We will never know and wholeheartedly do the will of God until we _____ (see p. 38).
7. In what ways is unity of attitude attained (see pp. 39-41)?
8. To think alike, what do we need to turn our thoughts away from (see p. 39)?

9. In situations of conflict, there will always be someone who is dwelling on the _____ (see p. 39).
10. True or false—To think with sound, divine judgment means to think subjectively (see p. 39). Explain your answer.
11. Those who are spiritually mature are in harmony with what (see p. 40)?
12. When will right relationships in the church exist (see p. 40)?
13. What happens when people fail to think on a divine level (see p. 41)?
14. What did Paul mean by the phrase "maintaining the same love" (see p. 41)?
15. What happens when people feel something other than love for each other (see p. 42)?
16. What is unique about the Greek word *sumpsuchoi*? What does it mean (see p. 42)?
17. What are some evidences of unity (see pp. 43-44)?

Pondering the Principles

1. In John 17:20-23 our Lord prays for the unity of believers. Often we think unity is something we must bring about, not something that *is*. But Jesus said it is God Himself who produces unity, a unity that exists only among people who have been born again. Martyn Lloyd-Jones, commenting on John 17, wrote, "There is no unity at all in our Lord's sense apart from this fundamental operation of the Holy Spirit of God who creates within the believers of the truth this new nature. And that in turn leads, by the same analogy, to an identity of view, of object, of love. . . . It is like a family relationship. You have no choice about that and what it involves. You are born into a family. Though you may disagree with members of your family, you cannot get rid of that relationship. It is a matter of blood and of essence. So is the unity of the Church. It must never be thought of, therefore, as something voluntary. It is something which is inevitable because it is the result of being born into a given family. Christians are brothers and not merely an association of friends" (*The Basis of Christian Unity* [Grand Rapids: Eerdmans, 1962], p. 14). How do you view fellow Christians—as acquaintances you could essentially do without or as brothers and sisters of the same family having the same Father (Eph. 4:6)?

2. Richard Baxter wrote, "A Christian indeed can bear the infirmities of the weak: though he love not their weakness, yet he pities it, because he truly loves their persons. Christ hath taught him not 'to break the bruised reed, and to gather the lambs in his arms, and carry them in his bosom, and gently lead them that are with young.' If they have diseases and distempers, he seeks in tenderness to cure them, and not in wrath to hurt and vex them. He turns not the infants or sick persons from the family, because they cry, or are unquiet, unclean, infirm, and troublesome; but he exercises his love and pity upon their weaknesses. If they mistake their way, or are ignorant, peevish, and [stubborn] in their mistakes, he seeks not to undo them, but gently to reduce them. If they censure him, and call him erroneous, heretical, antichristian, idolatrous, because he concurs not with them in their mistakes, he bears it with love and patience, as he would do the peevish chidings of a child, or the [grouchiness] of the sick. He doth not lose his charity, and set his wit against a child, or aggravate the crimes, and being reviled revile again; and say, you are schismatics, hypocrites, obstinate, and fit to be severely dealt with: but he overcomes them with love and patience, which is the conquest of a saint, and the happiest victory both for himself and them. 'It is a small matter to be judged of man.' He is more troubled for the weakness and disease of the censorious, than for his own being wronged by their censures" (*The Practical Works of Richard Baxter* [Grand Rapids: Baker, 1981 reprint], p. 735). Do you seek unity in the church with that kind of love?

4
The Means to Spiritual Unity

Outline

Review
I. The Motives for Unity (vv. 1-2*a*)
II. The Marks of Unity (v. 2*b*)

Lesson
III. The Means to Unity (vv. 3-4)
   A. Don't Be Selfish
   B. Don't Be Conceited
   C. Regard Others as More Important than Yourself
   D. Don't Look Out Only for Your Own Interests
   E. Be Concerned About Others' Interests

Conclusion

Review

I. THE MOTIVES FOR UNITY (vv. 1-2*a*; see pp. 26-31)

II. THE MARKS OF UNITY (v. 2*b*; see pp. 37-44)

Lesson

III. THE MEANS TO UNITY (vv. 3-4)

"Do nothing from selfishness or empty conceit, but with humility of mind let each of you regard one another as more im-

portant than himself; do not merely look out for your own personal interests, but also for the interests of others."

In that passage are five interrelated and practical principles describing the means to unity. Three are stated negatively, and two are positive. Obedience always has a negative and a positive side—what we must avoid and what we must do. These principles will help us examine our internal processes of thinking and motivation.

A. Don't Be Selfish

Christians are not to have selfish motives. Although no verb appears in the Greek text, Paul's statement has the force of a negative command: never act out of *eritheian*, which means "selfish ambition." It is sometimes translated "strife" because selfishness puts a person at war with others. It refers to factionalism, rivalry, and partisanship. Galatians 5:20 lists it as a work of the flesh.

Selfishness is egotism—a personal desire to advance one's self that is always destructive and disruptive. Unity in the church starts with slaying the giant of selfishness. Christians need to rid themselves of the consuming and destructive pride rooted deep in their fallen flesh. It's what prompts us to push for our own way and seek to fulfill our own agendas. The Greek word following *eritheian*—translated "empty conceit"—intensifies the picture of factionalism that Paul wanted the Philippians to avoid.

Factionalism was a problem in the Corinthian church. In 1 Corinthians 1:10 Paul says, "I exhort you, brethren, by the name of our Lord Jesus Christ, that you all agree, and there be no divisions among you." That factionalism showed itself as people in the church divided into parties: "Each one of you is saying, 'I am of Paul,' and 'I of Apollos,' and 'I of Cephas,' and 'I of Christ.'" We don't know what caused the Corinthians to divide up on the surface, but we do know that by doing so they evidenced a partisan, isolationist mentality. In chapter 3 Paul sums up the spiritual state of the Corinthians this way: "Since there is jealousy and strife among you, are you not fleshly, and are you not walking like mere men?" (v. 3). That reflects Paul's statement in Galatians 5:20 that selfishness is a work of the flesh.

The flesh produces selfishness, and unless we keep it under control, we can become consumed with our own agendas. Those agendas of themselves may be valid, but if compelled by selfishness they become competitive. That will produce jealousy, strife, and conflict—the end result being a loss of unity. As you deal with selfishness in your life, you'll begin to realize that you must consider more than your own goals.

B. Don't Be Conceited

The Greek word translated "empty conceit" (*kenodoxia*) is used only here in the New Testament. The King James Version translates it "vainglory." It refers to seeking after personal glory. "Selfishness" describes someone's pursuing an enterprise in a factional way, whereas "empty conceit" specifies the desired result: personal glory.

Kenodoxia is a compound word made up of *kenos* ("devoid of truth," "empty," "vain") and *doxa* ("glory"). A person whose character is reflected by that word assertively and arrogantly claims to be right but is in fact wrong. He holds an erroneous opinion of himself and the facts—all the while seeking his own glory. That kind of attitude creates discord. It's personal vanity.

C. Regard Others as More Important than Yourself

"With humility of mind let each of you regard one another as more important than himself" is a corrective for the negative commands given above. Unity is born out of humility.

"Humility of mind" translates one word from the Greek text of Philippians 2:3. It was apparently coined by the writers of the New Testament because it is not found in any previous ancient writings. The adjectival form of the word (Gk., *tapeinos*) was used in other Greek writings to describe the mentality of a slave. It conveyed the idea of being base, shabby, low, and common. It was a term of derision—not virtue. The pre–New Testament pagan world thought humility was something ugly, never to be sought, and certainly never to be admired.

But in the Old Testament God commends humility. He chose humble people to do His work. He saved the lowly and the meek. He hears the prayers of the downcast and gives grace to the lowly. So whereas humility is an affirmed virtue in the Old Testament, it was not so viewed in the pagan world. The writers of the New Testament were introducing their previously pagan readers to an entirely new concept.

Paul defined "humility of mind" as regarding one another more important than ourselves. We are to think of others in the church as superior to us. Yet often that's the opposite of what we think. For example, we're often quick to speak of the faults and failures of others.

Generally we can only guess what's in the heart of another. A wife may say to her husband, "I know what you're thinking," and she may or may not be right. If she's wrong, he may be frustrated, and if she's right, he may be even more frustrated! But it's generally true that the only sin or grace we know of in another person is what we see or hear. Yet there is one heart we all know very well—our own.

According to firsthand information, the worst sinner you know is yourself. We have so much data on our own sinfulness that we should have no problem considering others superior to ourselves, especially since all we tend to know about other people is what's on the outside.

That was Paul's attitude. We would probably say, "Paul, you're the greatest Christian who ever lived!" But he himself said, "I am the least of the apostles, who am not fit to be called an apostle" (1 Cor. 15:9) and, "Christ Jesus came into the world to save sinners, among whom I am foremost of all" (1 Tim. 1:15). According to his own knowledge of himself, Paul knew he was the worst sinner ever. And because of what we know of ourselves, we should adopt the same attitude toward ourselves. That should give you a different opinion of other people.

Discord, division, and factionalism end when we view others as more worthy of respect and honor, and more deserving to be heard and followed than ourselves. That's the attitude knowledge of our hearts ought to produce in us.

D. Don't Look Out Only for Your Own Interests

We live in a society where most people care only about their own personal interests. We're told to love ourselves, focus on ourselves, and even worship ourselves. But that only pours gasoline on the fire of human pride. In contrast, Paul said, "Do not merely look out for your own personal interests" (Phil. 2:4). "Look out for" speaks of regarding something as a goal. Christians aren't to regard their personal enterprises as their only goals in life. We are to be passionately involved in the causes of others. Often there's conflict because people are involved only with their piece of the pie—they don't see the big picture.

When he said "personal interests," I think Paul was speaking about legitimate ministry interests—those goals that honor the Lord and are part of our responsibilities as Christians. Those things are important, but our interests need to extend to the interests of others.

The word translated "interest" in the Greek text is a nonspecific term that has generated much discussion in commentaries regarding its meaning. It's likely that since the Lord inspired Paul to use a nonspecific term, that's the way we're to understand it. I think Paul meant that while we're busy tending to our responsibilities and other things on our hearts, we also need to be concerned about matters that concern those around us.

The interests, enterprises, needs, tasks, goals, gifts, spiritual character, ministries, qualities, strengths, and significance of others to the Lord and the church are to be considered equal in importance to our own. That's a high standard to live by. Competition in the Christian community is tragic.

E. Be Concerned About Others' Interests

We are to be concerned "for the interests of others" (Phil. 2:4). Other Christians have the right to our concern and prayers because they are important.

Conclusion

If the church lives by the standard of conduct God has set for us, we will eliminate competition and divisiveness. God's standard is very high. The only one who ever lived it to perfection was Jesus Christ, so He is our model (Phil. 2:5-8).

Focusing on the Facts

1. Obedience always has a negative and a positive side—what we must _____ and what we must _____ (see p. 48).
2. Christians are not to have _____ motives (see p. 48).
3. What is the meaning of the Greek word *eritheian* (see p. 48)?
4. What does selfishness prompt us to do (see p. 48)?
5. How did factionalism show itself in the church in Corinth (see p. 48)?
6. What is the meaning of the Greek word *kenodoxia* (see p. 49)?
7. Unity is born out of _____ (see p. 49).
8. What did the pre–New Testament pagan world think about humility (see pp. 49-50)?
9. How did Paul define humility of mind (see p. 50)?
10. What did Paul think about himself based on what he knew from firsthand experience (see p. 50)?
11. What kind of attitude should our knowledge about ourselves produce in us (see pp. 50-51)?
12. As Christians, what are we to be passionately involved in (see p. 51)?
13. Competition in the Christian community is _____ (see p. 51).

Pondering the Principles

1. Our time often views the mission of the church as that of a general peacemaker. But Martyn Lloyd-Jones observed that the program outlined in Philippians 2 "is only possible to the Christian; it is useless for the world outside. There is nothing that is so utterly idiotic as to ask men and women who are spiritually dead because of sin, to be humble and to think of others before themselves. They are incapable of such an action because before they can implement the Apostle's teaching, they must be born again" (*The Life of Joy* [Grand Rapids: Baker, 1989], p. 145). With that in mind, ask yourself these questions:

   - *As I seek to put off selfishness, act with humility, and prefer others before myself, am I doing so in my own strength or God's—am I truly born again?*

   - *In seeking to be a peacemaker in my circle of influence, am I always seeking first to see others reconciled to God, since that's the only way true peace can be established?*

2. Writing on Christian contentment, Puritan preacher Jeremiah Burroughs said, "One who creeps low cannot fall far, but it is those who are on high whose fall bruises them most. That is a good rule: do not promise yourself great things, neither aim at any great things in the world" (*The Rare Jewel of Christian Contentment* [Edinburgh: Banner of Truth Trust, 1964 reprint], p. 221). To prefer others is to cultivate an attitude of humility and deference in all of life. Are you aiming at great things for yourself, or for God and His people?

5
The Model for Spiritual Unity

Outline

Introduction
A. The Passage
B. Its Purpose
    1. An exhortation to the church
    2. An example to follow

Review
  I. The Motives for Unity (vv. 1-2*a*)
 II. The Marks of Unity (v. 2*b*)
III. The Means to Unity (vv. 3-4)

Lesson
IV. The Model for Unity (vv. 5-8)
    A. Jesus Was God (v. 6*a*)
    B. Jesus Did Not Cling to His Equality with God (v. 6*b*)
    C. Jesus Emptied Himself (v. 7*a*)
        1. He gave up His heavenly glory
        2. He gave up His independent authority
        3. He gave up the prerogatives of His divine nature
        4. He gave up His eternal riches
        5. He gave up His favorable relationship with God
    D. Jesus Became a Servant (v. 7*b*)
    E. Jesus Identified with Sinners (v. 7*c*)
    F. Jesus Looked Like a Man (v. 8*a*)
    G. Jesus Humbled Himself (v. 8*b*)
    H. Jesus Was Obedient to the Point of Death (v. 8*b*)
    I. Jesus Died on a Cross (v. 8*c*)

Conclusion

Introduction

The Greek text of Philippians 2:5-8 hints that the passage was probably a hymn of the early church. No other New Testament passage so completely details the event of God's becoming man in Christ Jesus. Theologians have called it a Christological gem—a sparkling diamond of the New Testament.

A. The Passage

Paul said to "have this attitude in yourselves which was also in Christ Jesus, who, although He existed in the form of God, did not regard equality with God a thing to be grasped, but emptied Himself, taking the form of a bond-servant, and being made in the likeness of men. And being found in appearance as a man, He humbled Himself by becoming obedient to the point of death, even death on a cross."

B. Its Purpose

1. An exhortation to the church

Whereas that passage is a strong, unfathomable, theological statement on the nature of Christ, its main intent is ethical. The context reveals that Paul was trying to motivate believers to live out their faith.

2. An example to follow

God's becoming man is the supreme illustration of humility. Philippians 2:5-8 is a living portrait of self-sacrifice, self-denial, self-giving, and boundless love. Christ was the perfect, ethical illustration of humility.

a) Matthew 11:29—He said, "Take My yoke upon you, and learn from Me, for I am gentle and humble in heart."

b) John 13:34—After washing His disciples' feet, Jesus said, "A new commandment I give to you, that you love one another, even as I have loved you, that you

also love one another." How had Jesus loved them?
By His humble service—He washed their dirty feet.

In Philippians 2:6-8 Paul chronicles the descent of Christ from His
lofty, heavenly position to His humble, earthly estate.

Review

Lesson

IV. THE MODEL FOR UNITY (vv. 5-8)

Philippians 2:5 says, "Have this attitude in yourselves which
was also in Christ Jesus." Paul wanted the Philippians to see
our Lord as a model for the kind of attitude that would foster
unity in the church—the unity he just exhorted them to in
verses 1-4. The humility of Christ provides the ultimate model
for unity in the church.

A. Jesus Was God (v. 6a)

"He existed in the form of God."

The Greek word translated "form" refers to one's nature,
essence, or innate being. Christ is God, and He preexisted
in the form of God before the incarnation. That tells us the
starting point of Christ's humiliation. He stooped from the
high point of possessing the being of God. His descent into
humility was far greater than we will ever know because
we never were and never will be God.

Even though we cannot know the kind of humiliation
Christ experienced, He nonetheless is a model to follow.

We are the children of God—His sons and daughters. We are blessed with all spiritual blessings in the heavenlies in Christ Jesus (Eph. 1:3). We are the chosen and beloved, and we are anointed by the Holy Spirit. We are a special people who have been given the promise of heaven's eternal glory. We serve as priests and chosen vessels, are ambassadors of Christ, and enjoy the exalted position of being sons of God indwelt by the Spirit of God. Therefore, our humiliation begins from a lofty level as well. Humiliation begins with a recognition of the lofty starting point from which we are required to descend for the benefit of others.

B. Jesus Did Not Cling to His Equality with God (v. 6b)

"He . . . did not regard equality with God a thing to be grasped."

This second step in the humiliation of Christ helps explain His being "in the form of God." That and "equality with God" (v. 6b) mean the same thing. The Greek word *isos*, translated "equality," refers to an exact equal.

Although He was equal with God, Jesus did not regard that position as "a thing to be grasped." Loftiness of calling is not something to be grasped. It is not to be clenched as a prized possession, to be selfishly exploited and never set aside for the benefit of another.

You will see the humility of Christ in you when you begin to loosen your grip on the privileges and possessions you have as a believer. As God, Christ was in a favored position with unimaginable privileges. His position was infinitely perfect and infinitely fulfilling. He was worthy of it and could not be disqualified from it. But His attitude was not to cling to His position if by letting go He could serve another.

C. Jesus Emptied Himself (v. 7a)

"[He] emptied Himself."

Christ's attitude of not grasping His privileges and position led to His action of emptying Himself. He divested Himself of His privileges, letting go of His position as He descend-

58

ed into a humble, human state. He didn't cease to be God—that's clear in the New Testament. While on earth Christ clearly claimed to be God: "He who has seen Me has seen the Father" (John 14:9; cf. 10:30-33). Christ remained fully God but emptied Himself of His privileges and position to descend to the desperate level of unworthy sinners.

1. He gave up His heavenly glory

    Shortly before His mission came to a close, Jesus prayed, "Now, glorify Thou Me together with Thyself, Father, with the glory which I had with Thee before the world was" (John 17:5). That verse shows that Christ must have given up His heavenly glory. He longed for a *pros ton theon* ("face to face with God") relationship , as the apostle John called it in John 1:1. Jesus often prayed because He loved intimate communion with the Father—a heavenly glory He had given up for a time.

2. He gave up His independent authority

    Christ gave up the independent authority He had as God and learned obedience (Heb. 5:8). He said, "I can do nothing on My own initiative. As I hear, I judge; and My judgment is just, because I do not seek My own will, but the will of Him who sent Me" (John 5:30).

3. He gave up the prerogatives of His divine nature

    He gave up the prerogatives of His divine nature, voluntarily limiting His divine attributes. He didn't even know when the Father would set up His kingdom (Matt. 24:36). He said no man knew—not even the Son. He willingly set aside the exercise of His divine attribute of omniscience.

4. He gave up His eternal riches

    He set aside His eternal riches. It is impossible to fully grasp how rich Christ was. Second Corinthians 8:9 says, "He was rich, yet for your sake He became poor." He was so poor that He said, "The foxes have holes, and the birds of the air have nests; but the Son of Man has nowhere to lay His head" (Matt. 8:20).

5. He gave up His favorable relationship with God

On the cross Jesus cried, "My God, My God, why hast Thou forsaken Me?" (Matt. 27:46). He experienced alienation from the triune God of whom He was part. God the Father "made Him who knew no sin [God the Son] to be sin on our behalf, that we might become the righteousness of God" (2 Cor. 5:21).

Christ gave up a great deal—but that's what the humble person does. According to Paul, our humility is to be like Christ's: though we recognize our rights and privileges, we are not to grasp after those things. Ours is to be a humility that sees the needs of another and is willing to divest itself and stoop, if necessary, to meet those needs.

D. Jesus Became a Servant (v. 7*b*)

"[He took] the form of a bond-servant."

The humility of Christ extended to the point of slavery. Christ's servitude was not theatrical. It was not make-believe. He didn't put on the garment of a slave; He actually became one. Verse 6 says He "existed in the form of God," and verse 7 says He took "the form of a bond-servant." "Form" means "essential character" in both verses. Jesus took on the essential character of a slave.

1. Luke 22:27—Jesus said, "I am among you as the one who serves."

2. Matthew 20:28—"The Son of Man did not come to be served, but to serve, and to give His life a ransom for many."

3. Isaiah 53:6—"The Lord has caused the iniquity of us all to fall on Him." Slaves carry burdens. Jesus Christ carried the greatest burden any slave could ever carry: the burden of the sin of humanity.

E. Jesus Identified with Sinners (v. 7*c*)

"[He was] made in the likeness of men."

Christ's service to sinners took the form of total identification with them. He became like us. He had all the attributes of a man. He was a genuine human—not just a facsimile.

When God became man in the form of Jesus Christ, He did not become man as man was before the Fall. He partook of human nature in its fallen and weakened condition: He hurt, He wept, He hungered, He thirsted, He tired, and He died. He was burdened with the results of man's Fall (cf. William Hendriksen, *New Testament Commentary: Exposition of Philippians* [Grand Rapids: Baker, 1962], p. 110).

When Christ took on human nature in its fallen character, it was with one significant element eliminated: sin. Jesus was "tempted in all things as we are, yet without sin" (Heb. 4:15). Although Christ never sinned, He felt the results of the Fall when He became one of us. Otherwise, He could not have been tempted in all things as we are and be our sympathetic High Priest (Heb. 4:15). Christ walked in our skin. His sympathy for us is our model of humility.

F. Jesus Looked Like a Man (v. 8*a*)

"[He was] found in appearance as a man."

The next step in Christ's descent relates closely to Paul's statement at the end of verse 7, which affirms the fact of the incarnation. Verse 8 views the incarnation from the vantage point of the people who saw and experienced Him. Christ was so much like man that those who knew Him thought Him to be no different from themselves. Obviously, those who knew Jesus didn't think He was condescending to them. They rightly felt that Christ understood them because He appeared to be just like them. His appearance as a man was so authentic that most of them couldn't tell who He really was. He so closely identified with them as man that they thought Him no better than themselves. That's a tragedy on the one hand, but it is a profound illustration of humility on the other.

G. Jesus Humbled Himself (v. 8*b*)

"He humbled Himself."

The humility of Christ went beyond His identification with mankind. Christ didn't ask for a palace, a chariot, servants, a wardrobe, or jewelry. He lived and appeared as a simple man. The God who made the universe stood alongside a man named Joseph and helped him in his carpenter shop in Nazareth. What humility!

H. Jesus Was Obedient to the Point of Death (v. 8*b*)

"[He became] obedient to the point of death."

Yet His humility extended far beyond His poverty and simple way of life. Christ's humility was such that He was willing to die for sinners: "Greater love has no one than this, that one lay down his life for his friends" (John 15:13). Christ volunteered to die—no man took His life from Him (John 10:18). He gave Himself up to an undeserved death and died the death of humility personified.

Christ stooped to die for sinners because that was the way sinful men and women had to be served. There was no other way to deliver them since "the wages of sin is death" (Rom. 6:23). God's holiness required that His wrath be satisfied, and that required a sacrifice. For Christ to help sinful man meant that He would have to die in the sinner's place and pay the penalty for sin.

I. Jesus Died on a Cross (v. 8*c*)

"Even death on a cross."

The humility of Christ extended even to death—but what a death! The final step in the humiliation of Christ was the kind of death He suffered. Of the many ways a man could die, Christ experienced the most torturous death mankind has ever devised. He suffered incredible pain, shame, nakedness, and disgrace. He was spit on, punched, and jeered at. And most crushing of all, He actually became sin and was deserted by God.

Conclusion

Sometimes humility is painful and sometimes it's unfair. Often it's misunderstood, and usually it's costly. Jesus provides the example of the kind of humility we are called to model. We often say, "If only we had unity in our church!" But unity comes only at a high price: Christlike humility. There are no shortcuts or quick fixes. Unity in the church comes only when its members serve each other as Christ served all. Philippians 2:5-8 is a passage not only about Christ but about what we are to be.

Focusing on the Facts

1. According to the context, why did Paul write Philippians 2:5-8 (see p. 56)?
2. God's becoming man is a supreme illustration of _____ (see p. 56).
3. Even though we cannot know the kind of humiliation Christ experienced, He nonetheless is a _____ to follow (see p. 57).
4. What was the starting point of Christ's humiliation (see p. 57)?
5. What does the Greek word *isos* mean? Why is it important that we recognize that word's exact meaning (see p. 58)?
6. What do believers need to loosen their grip on (see p. 58)?
7. When Christ became a man, did He cease to be God? Support your answer from Scripture (see p. 59).
8. What precisely did Christ empty Himself of (see pp. 59-60)?
9. When Christ took "the form of a bond-servant," was it a true transformation or only external? Why or why not (see p. 60)?
10. When God became Man in Christ, what exactly did He partake of in terms of human characteristics (see p. 61)?
11. Did the people around Jesus think He was human? Explain (see p. 61).
12. Why did Christ stoop to die for sinners (see p. 62)?

Pondering the Principles

1. The humility of Christ came at a terrible cost to Him. Writing of his resolve to follow our Lord's humble example, Jonathan Edwards wrote, "Now, henceforth, I am not to act, in any respect, as my own.—I shall act as my own, if I ever make use of any of my powers to do any thing that is not to the glory of God, and do not make the glorifying of Him my whole and entire business:—if I murmur in the least at affliction; if I grieve at the prosperity of others; if I am in any way uncharitable; if I am angry because of injuries; if I revenge them; if I do anything purely to please myself, or avoid any thing for the sake of my own ease; if I omit anything because it is great self-denial; if I trust to myself; or I take any of the praise of the good that I do, or that God doth by me; or if I am in any way proud" (*The Works of Jonathan Edwards* [Edinburgh: Banner of Truth Trust, 1974], p. xxv). Christ gave His all for you—have you given your all to Him?

2. The Puritan William Bridge wrote, "Glorious is the fellowship and communion that the saints have with Christ. . . . They have not only fellowship with him in his sufferings, to have suffering for suffering; but they have fellowship in his graces, grace for grace; and this fellowship hath the Father brought you into" (*The Works of the Reverend William Bridge,* vol. 1 [Beaver Falls, Pa.: Soli Deo Gloria, 1989 reprint], p. 289). Often we struggle for unity with our eyes fixed upon each other, forgetting that we all belong to Christ, who is our model. As you seek unity in your church, remember that your self-denial for the sake of unity is pleasing to Christ, who died that we might be conformed to His image (Rom. 8:29).

Scripture Index

Topical Index

Affection, of Christ. *See* Jesus Christ
Amusing Ourselves to Death. *See* Postman, Neil
Arn, Win, on the church cycle of decline, 18

Barclay, William, on disunity, 24
Baxter, Richard
   on bearing infirmities, 46
   on the sins of pastors, 21
Bridge, William, on fellowship with Christ, 64
Burroughs, Jeremiah, on humility, 53

Church, the
   conduct of, 7-21
   cycle of decline, 18-19
   integrity of, 10-12, 21
   unity of (*see* Unity)
Citizenship, heavenly, 8-9
Compassion, of the Holy Spirit. *See* Holy Spirit
Compromise, unity versus. *See* Unity

Disunity. *See* Unity

Edwards, Jonathan
   on glorifying God, 64
   profundity of, 17-18
   on religious affections, 64
Encouragement, in Christ. *See* Jesus Christ
Entertainment, excessive. *See* Postman, Neil

Fallen leaders. *See* Leadership

Finney, Charles G., profundity of, 17

God, love of. *See* Jesus Christ, love of
Grace Community Church
   church cycle of decline and, 18-19
   unity and, 24, 36

"Health and wealth" movement, suffering and the, 19-20
Hendriksen, William, on Christ's becoming man, 61
Holy Spirit, the
   affection of, 29-30
   compassion of, 30-31
   fellowship of, 28
Humility
   cost of, 62-64
   marks of, 35-46
   means to, 47-54
   model of, 55-64

Integrity, of the church. *See* Church

Jesus Christ
   appearance of, 61
   deity of, 57-58
   encouragement in, 26-27
   equality with God, 58
   essence of, 57-58
   example of, 55-64
   humiliation of, 55-64
   incarnation of, 55-64
   love of, 27-28
   privileges of, 58-60